# Acknowledgements

We would like to thank our editorial advisers, Pat Charlesworth, Nigel Hollins and the Women's Group at Blakes & Link Employment Agency, for helping us to think of ideas for this book and for telling us what was needed in the pictures. We would also like to thank all those bereavement counsellors and their clients in Merton, Wandsworth, Bognor, Edinburgh and Inverness who also had ideas about what was needed in the pictures.

We were very lucky to have representatives on the book's Advisory Group from Cruse Bereavement Care and St George's Hospital Medical School. We would like to thank Paul Adeline, Rosie Dalzell and Jane Hubert for their time which they gave most generously. Thanks also to Dorothea Duncan for her continuing commitment to the series.

Our grateful thanks go to roc and Hertfordshire Partnership NHS Trust for releasing Noelle Blackman to work on this book as a co-author.

Finally, we are grateful to the Communities of L'Arche for their partnership in the Community Fund research project which helped to make this book possible.

# When Somebody Dies

**Sheila Hollins, Sandra Dowling
and Noelle Blackman,
illustrated by Catherine Brighton**

**Books Beyond Wo**

**Gaskell/St George's Hospital Medical School**

**LONDON**

First published in Great Britain 2003 by Gaskell and St George's Hospital Medical School.

Text & illustration © Sheila Hollins & Catherine Brighton 2003.

ISBN 1-901242-90-0

British Library Cataloguing-in-Publication Data

A catalogue record for this book is available from the British Library.

Distributed in North America by Balogh International Inc.

Printed and bound in Great Britain by Specialblue Limited, London.

Gaskell is a registered trademark of The Royal College of Psychiatrists.

Further information about the Books Beyond Words series can be obtained from:

Royal College of Psychiatrists
17 Belgrave Square
London SW1X 8PG
Tel: 020 7235 2351
Fax: 020 7245 1231

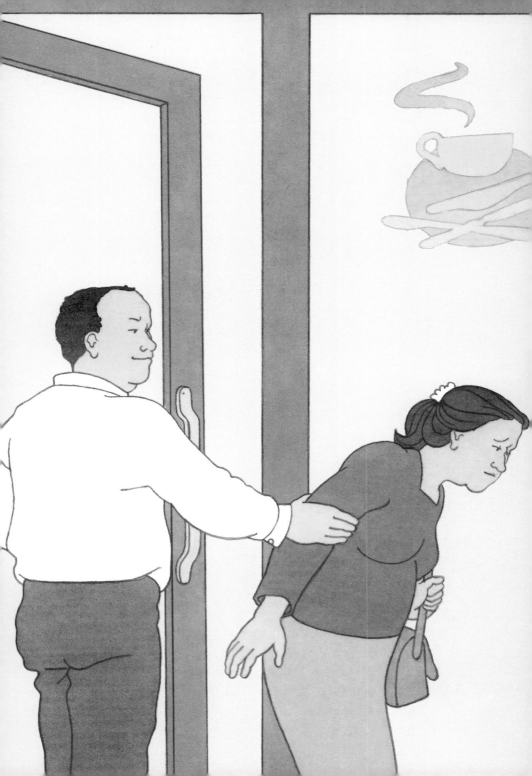

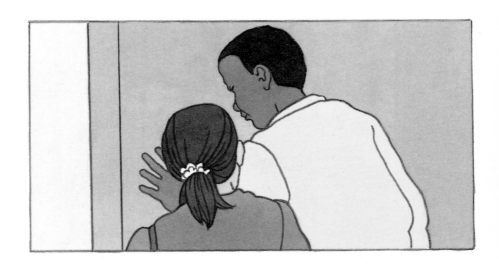

19

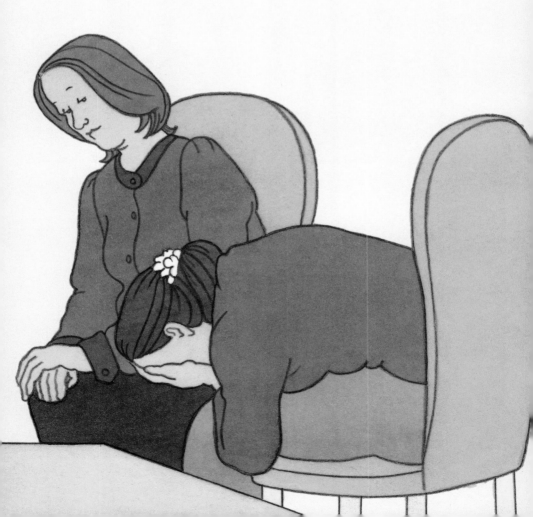

23

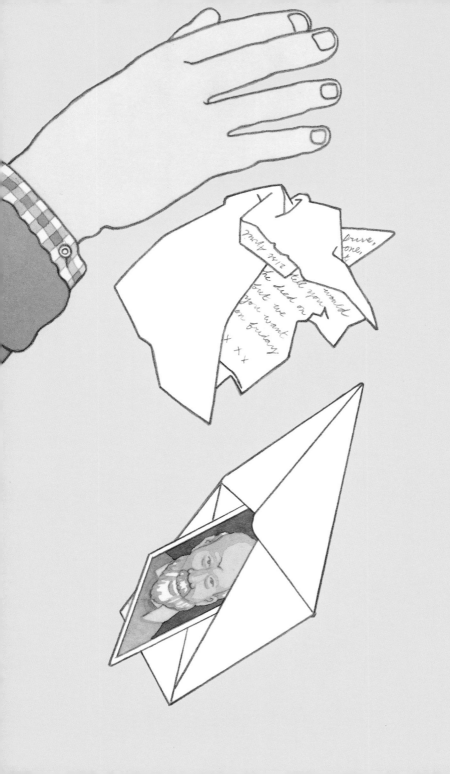

# The following words are provided for people who want a ready-made story rather than to tell their own

1. Mary and Frank have been to a funeral. They both look very upset.

2. On the way home they meet the postman and a neighbour. Frank says hello. Mary just looks away. She is feeling sad.

3. Mary and Frank are sitting on the sofa. There are lots of photographs of family and friends on the sideboard. Frank is watching TV. Mary is looking away. She is sad and can't concentrate. The cat is sleeping on her knee.

4. Mary is crying. She is on her own in the kitchen. She has been looking at a photograph. She misses the person in the picture. She has no one to talk to.

5. Frank tries to comfort Mary but she is still crying. Mary turns away. She holds the picture close to her.

6. Frank is hiding the picture from Mary. He thinks this will help because Mary gets upset when she looks at it. Mary sees him from the door.

7. Mary is cross. She comes into the room and shouts at Frank. She yells, "leave the picture out of the drawer". Frank doesn't know what to say.

8. Frank leaves the room. Mary is alone. She is thinking about her photo.

9. Frank has gone to a café. He looks worried. A friend is with him. He might be able to help.

10. Frank tells his friend that Mary is sad because someone has died. He says he wants to help but doesn't know how. Frank's friend listens carefully.

11. Frank has brought a pizza home. He wants to cheer Mary up.

12. Mary and Frank share the pizza. Mary is looking a little better. She is glad that Frank is trying to help her.

13. Frank takes Mary to the café. She is worried but Frank says lets go in, you will be OK.

14. Mary, Frank and their friend are in the café. They are talking about how to help Mary to feel better. Mary says she is having a difficult time.

15. Mary talks to their friend about how she is feeling. She tells him that someone she loves has died. He has an idea about what might help.

16. The friend telephones a bereavement counsellor. He makes an appointment for Mary.

17a. Mary's friend takes her to meet the counsellor.

17. Mary is introduced to the counsellor. The counsellor seems very nice.

18. The counsellor explains how she can help. Mary can tell the counsellor about how she is feeling. The counsellor will listen to Mary, and help her to remember the person who has died.

19a. Mary visits the counsellor again.

19. Mary cries. The counsellor understands. She lets Mary cry. This helps her to feel better.

20a. Mary arrives for her counselling appointment.

20. Mary brings some photographs to show to the counsellor. She is talking about her memories. Mary says she misses the person who died.

21a. Mary has come for counselling again. It is winter now. She has been coming since the summertime.

21. Mary feels upset when she sees the counsellor. She listens to what Mary says. She really understands.

22. Mary goes to the grave with the counsellor. She has brought some flowers. She wants to put the flowers on the grave.

23. Mary is feeling much better. She is smiling. She is at home with Frank having breakfast. He is glad that Mary feels better.

24. The postman brings a letter for Frank.

25 Frank opens his letter. It is bad news. Frank is shocked.

26. Frank crushes the letter. He drops it. A photograph falls out.

27. Frank shows the photograph to Mary. She puts her arm around him. She knows how it feels when someone dies. Mary comforts Frank.

28. Frank is alone. He is looking out of the window. He is holding the photograph in his hand. He looks sad.

29. Frank and Mary look through this book together. Mary is helping Frank by talking to him and comforting him.

30. Mary and Frank go to the funeral together. Their friends are there too. Frank is very sad.

31. Frank, Mary and their friends are together. They are talking about the person who has died. They know how to help each other. They are trying to support one another.

32. Mary and Frank leave to go home. They both look sad. Perhaps it reminds Mary of her own bereavement.

33. Mary and Frank put photographs into an album. These will help them to remember the people who have died.

34. Frank is feeling a little better. He has done some shopping. He talks to his neighbour on the way home.

35. Frank sees Mary in the café talking to their friend.

36. Frank decides to join Mary and their friend. Mary and Frank look happy now.

# What is grief?

When somebody dies we experience many different emotions. Sometimes people say they feel numb and helpless. They may be shocked and overwhelmed by the news. Often it is difficult to take in what has happened; "I just can't believe it" some may say over and over.

People may feel angry with doctors, nurses or carers. They may blame others for the death. They may also be angry with the person who has died, for leaving them. Some bereaved people feel guilty, or regretful about things that happened before the death. People often say they feel overwhelmingly sad. They may yearn for their loved ones or even search for them, half-expecting to see them again. People may become withdrawn, or have difficulty sleeping or finding peace of mind during the day. This is grief.

People grieve in different ways. Every society and culture has its own way of dealing with death. It is important to be familiar with rituals which are relevant locally.

While some of our grief is shared with other people, other aspects are more personal. Commonly, people will visit the grave of their loved one, or the site where ashes were placed. There may be days when memories are especially acute such as birthdays or other special anniversaries.

Listening to music, visiting a favourite place, or taking up activities enjoyed by the person who has died, are just some ways that help people to remember and to grieve. Some people think that death changes a relationship rather than ends it. They may continue to talk to their friend or relative while looking at a photograph or by the grave. They may say things they wish had been said before the death, or simply tell the person who has died about everyday happenings. Others may write letters or a journal as a way of maintaining a bond. For some people, this can be very comforting and an important part of their personal grieving.

# What happens to people with learning disabilities when somebody dies?

It is sometimes hard to describe our feelings to other people, especially as they do not always know what to do or say to help. For someone with a learning disability this can be even more difficult. One thing that adds to this difficulty is the attitude of society. For instance, in the past many people with learning disabilities were not told when someone died. It was often thought that they would not understand or that they would get too upset. We know now that it is better to tell people if someone dies. It is vital to be sensitive to people's feelings when telling bad news and it should be done by someone who knows them well.

People are likely to be upset when they hear that someone they love has died. This is perfectly natural and should not be ignored or stifled.

Inclusion is important, not just immediately after the death, but in the following months and years. Many people with learning disabilities do not have the opportunity to grieve in a personal way. They may never have gone to visit the cemetery, but when given the chance many are keen to do so.

Often people do not have any mementos or even photographs to help them to remember. Some people's memories may be sketchy, and if details have not been recorded, their pasts may be unknown to the people who know them now.

Remembering is an important part of grieving, so it is vital that memories are available to people with learning disabilities. Life-story books, memory boxes or a family tree are useful ways of recording a person's life history in a way that is accessible. This may help people not only to cope with death but also to enjoy life.

If people are not given the chance to be involved in the collective activities of grief, or they are not supported to grieve in a personal way, it can become difficult for them to find ways to understand their loss.

People may not have had the chance to learn ways to express their feelings. By being kept away from funerals, wakes or other rituals and by not sharing in the feelings of their grieving relatives, many will have missed out on the opportunity to learn how others behave, in their cultural setting, following a death.

We all learn how to play our part from watching others, but people with learning disabilities are somehow expected to know what happens, without having had the chance to learn. Some people find it hard to communicate their thoughts and ideas to others, and it may also be hard for them to understand what others tell them.

It is important that carers, family members and friends talk to bereaved people about what has happened and how they are feeling, and that they try to find out what they can do to help. This may only mean taking a little extra time and care, and being aware of the bereaved person's feelings.

Grief can last for a long time, several months or several years. This depends on the nature of the loss and on individual responses to it.

No one should be expected to feel 'better' after just a few weeks. Also, feelings of grief may subside for a time and then reappear later, and at such times particular care and understanding are needed.

Emotional distress may be shown through the way people behave. They may become withdrawn or agitated, they may be aggressive or unusually passive, or there may be other changes in the way they act. Others may not realise that these changes are related to their bereavement. They may be labelled as having 'challenging behaviour', and services may be designed around this label, while the loss and pain go unnoticed.

It is very important that carers, family members and friends are aware that changes in behaviour could be an expression of feelings, however recent or distant their loss.

## Does bereavement counselling work with people with learning disabilities?

A new research study tried to find the answer to the question 'What helps a person with learning disabilities when someone close to them dies?' The research found that counselling helps people to feel better. It was not enough to ask support workers and family carers to provide extra help and understanding. Copies of the research report are available at £5 (inc. p&p) from the Department of Mental Health – Learning Disability, St George's Hospital Medical School, Jenner Wing, Cranmer Terrace, London SW17 0RE. Tel: 020 8725 5496; fax: 020 8672 1070.

# Counselling someone with a learning disability

Many counsellors feel that they do not have the skills to work with someone who has a learning disability, although those who have done so find that it is really very similar to counselling anyone else. Some adjustments to a counsellor's usual way of working may be needed when working with someone who has a learning disability, according to their individual needs. The following pages give some points to consider.

# Communication

Find out about how a client prefers to communicate before you begin to work together. You could ask the client, or whoever referred them for counselling.

If the client has limited verbal communication skills, it may be helpful for someone who knows them well to accompany them to the sessions, to help you to understand one another. You may need to simplify your language and support what you say with signs and symbols, or to emphasise your facial expressions.

If someone's speech is unclear you may find that it becomes easier to understand what the person is saying as time goes by.

Some people may say very little. They may be shy or think that no one is concerned with what they have to say. It might be unusual for someone else to be interested in their thoughts and feelings. It may, therefore, be difficult for people to tell you what they think or how they feel.

Their reticence does not necessarily mean that they do not understand what you are saying. Do continue to talk and share your thoughts and ideas. As you get to know one another it is likely that your client will be able to communicate more freely with you.

Think about offering a wide range of communication techniques. Drawing and painting can be a good way for people to 'say' how they are feeling. Puppets or dolls can help someone to tell a story or to express something difficult. Other pictures and photographs can also be useful to supplement the pictures in this book (see the list of books and packs that can help with communication). Remember that no single way will work with everybody.

People with learning disabilities, perhaps because of a desire to please or a fear of getting something wrong, may respond in the way they think you want them to. It is important to try to word questions impartially, and to be aware of any signals that may influence your client's reply.

# Consent

It should never be assumed that people are not able to make their own decisions simply because they have a learning disability. An investment in time and communication with the person concerned and his or her carers is necessary. Information should be given to people in a straightforward way, using plain language, visual prompts, signs and symbols as required.

For further information about consent, see *Seeking Consent: Working with People with Learning Disabilities* (Department of Health, 2001).

Few people understand what counselling will involve before they have experienced it. If the person comes to the session willingly, it will be very clear after an initial assessment whether they want to come again. Others will try it and see. If someone shows an unwillingness to continue with sessions, he or she should be supported to withdraw from counselling in an appropriate and sensitive manner.

# Confidentiality

The confidentiality of the counselling situation is essentially the same when working with a client who has a learning disability as when working with any other client. However, you may become worried that your client is ill, is at risk from someone else, or is a risk to themselves or someone else.

It is important to discuss issues of confidentiality with your client at the outset. You could say something like this: "I will not tell anyone else what we talk about in our sessions, unless you say something that makes me worried about you. If I need to tell anyone about something you have said, we will talk about the best way to do this. I will not say anything to other people that you do not know about." If you discuss your sessions with a supervisor, you should mention this to your client.

# Where to find help and advice

**Cruse Bereavement Care** is the national organisation for bereaved people. Many counsellors are willing to work with people with learning disabilities.

Contact: Cruse Bereavement Care, Cruse House, 126 Sheen Road, Surrey TW9 1UR. Tel: 020 8939 9530.

**Day by Day** is the Cruse National Helpline 0870 167 1677; e-mail: Helpline@crusebereavementcare.co.uk. Provides support and information about local bereavement counselling services. Also gives welfare advice.

**Respond Helpline** 0800 808 0700. Supports people with learning disabilities, their carers and professionals around any issue of trauma, including bereavement.

It is often possible to access bereavement counselling through a GP, although this is often very short-term counselling. Many Community Teams for People with Learning Disabilities (CTPLDs) can offer bereavement counselling.

From 2005 everyone who has a learning disability will have a Health Action Plan. A bereavement need could be included in a person's Health Action Plan, which would then mean that he or she should be supported to get any help that they may need in order to access bereavement counselling.

For more information about Health Action Plans, see *Action for Health – Health Action Plans and Health Facilitation*, which contains detailed good practice guidance. This is available free from the Department of Health, PO Box 777, London SE1 6XH. An easy-to-read version for people with learning disabilities is also available.

It is worth contacting local bereavement counselling services (these should be listed in local directories) to find out whether they offer counselling to people with learning disabilities.

If they do not, this could be because they have not thought about it before. They may be prepared to counsel people with learning disabilities, but feel that they do not have enough knowledge. They might want to know more about what it means to have a learning disability and how they would need to adapt their skills. They may want to have some special training. This could be provided in a number of different ways.

- Some advocacy and self-advocacy groups offer training about learning disability.
- Some community teams for people with learning disabilities provide training.
- The training could be provided by a specialist training services such as roc (see below).

There are a few services nationally which specialise in offering bereavement counselling to people with learning disabilities. One such service is the **roc loss and bereavement service**, based within Hertfordshire Partnership NHS Trust. **roc** is only able to offer counselling to people living in Hertfordshire but can offer training in counselling nationally.

Contact: roc, Hertfordshire Partnership NHS Trust, Woodside Road, Abbots Langley, Hertfordshire WD5 0HT. Tel: 01923 663 628.

# Written information

*Am I allowed to Cry*? by Maureen Oswin. A study of bereavement among people who have learning difficulties. £12.99. Human Horizons series, Souvenir Press. Order through a bookshop.

*Exploring Your Emotions* by A. Holland, A. Payne and L. Vickery. A set of 30 full colour photographs illustrating common emotions that can be used in educational and therapeutic settings to help people with learning disabilities learn about their own feelings and the relationship between emotion and behaviour. £25.00, including a manual (+£2.50 p&p). British Institute of Learning Disabilities: distributed by Plymbridge Distributors Ltd; Tel: 01752 202 301; fax: 01752 202 333.

*Helping Adults with Mental Retardation Grieve a Death Loss* by Charlene Luchterhand and Nancy Murphy. Includes a list of 108 creative ideas for activities aimed at helping people cope with bereavement. £10.95. Accelerated Development (USA), available in UK through a bookseller from Taylor & Francis, London.

*Living with Loss: Helping People with Learning Disabilities Cope with Bereavement and Loss* edited by Noelle Blackman. £12.95 (+£3.50 p&p). Pavilion Publishing, 8 St George's Place, Brighton, Surrey BN1 4GB. Tel: 0870 161 3505; fax: 0870 161 3506.

*When Mum Died* and *When Dad Died* by Sheila Hollins and Lester Sireling. These two Books Beyond Words take an honest and straightforward approach to death and grief in the family. The pictures tell the story of the death of a parent in a simple but moving way. The third editions of these books, currently in press, contain new guidelines for carers, supporters and professionals. £10.00 each. Book Sales, Royal College of Psychiatrists, 17 Belgrave Square, London SW1 8PG. Tel: 020 7235 2351, ext 146.

*Understanding Death and Dying* by F. Cathcart. A series of three booklets that help someone with a learning disability to come to terms with bereavement: *Your Feelings* (illustrated): £3.50 (+£2.40 p&p); *A Guide for Families and Friends*: £4.00 (+£.2.50 p&p); and *A Guide for Carers and Other Professionals*: £4.00 (+£2.50 p&p). British Institute of Learning Disabilities (see previous page).

*Talking Together About Death* by J. Cooley and F. McGauran. A bereavement pack containing five sets of sensitively illustrated cards and a user's guide. Designed for both families and carers to share the experience of death and bereavement with people with learning disabilities. £52.82 (incl. VAT). Winslow Press, Telford Road, Bicester, Oxon OX6 0TS.

*Loss and Learning Disability* by Noelle Blackman. This book is for care staff, therapists and counsellors working with people with learning disabilities. It talks about how people with learning disabilities can be affected by bereavement. It includes ways to prevent normal grief from becoming a bigger problem, and ways of helping people when the grief process 'goes wrong'. Published by Worth Publishing Ltd, London at £16.99, and available to order from all good booksellers.

## Videos

*Coping with Death*. Explains what happens when somebody dies and shows adults with learning disabilities coping with death. £28.00 (incl. p&p). Speak Up Self Advocacy, 43 Holm Flatt Street, Parkgate, Rotherham, South Yorkshire S62 6HJ. Tel: 01709 7100199; fax: 01709 510009.

## Training pack

*Understanding Grief*: *Working with Grief and People Who Have Learning Disabilities* by Sheila Hollins and Lester Sireling. Can be used in formal staff training or as an education tool for families and carers of a bereaved person with learning disabilities. The pack includes a video *When People Die* and a copy of *When Dad Died*. £125.00 + VAT (total £146.88), +£3.50 p&p. Pavilion Publishing (see previous page for address).

# Other titles in the Books Beyond Words series

Using health services is explained in *Going to the Doctor, Going to Out-Patients* and *Going into Hospital. Looking After My Breasts* and *Keeping Healthy 'Down Below'* are about breast and cervical screening. *Getting On With Cancer* describes the experiences of a woman who has cancer.

Three books cover access to criminal justice as a victim (witness) or as a defendant: *Going to Court, You're Under Arrest* and *You're on Trial*.

*Mugged* tells what happens to a young man after he is attacked and robbed in the street.

The difficult subject of sexual abuse is covered in *Bob Tells All, Jenny Speaks Out* and *I Can Get Through It*. Counselling and psychotherapy after sexual abuse are explained in the third title.

*Feeling Blue* aims to help people to understand depression.

*Speaking Up for Myself* shows how people with learning disabilities from ethnic minority groups have the right to challenge discrimination.

Forming new relationships is the subject of *Making Friends* and *Hug Me, Touch Me*. The ups and downs of a romantic relationship are traced in *Falling in Love*.

Two books about personal care are *George Gets Smart* and *Susan's Growing Up.* The latter tells the story of a young girl's first menstruation.

*Food...Fun, Healthy and Safe* shows how choosing, cooking and eating food can be fun as well as healthy and safe.

To order copies (at £10.00 each; £9.00 each for 10 or more books) or for a leaflet giving more information, please contact: Book Sales, Royal College of Psychiatrists, 17 Belgrave Square, London SW1X 8PG. Credit card orders can be taken by telephone (020 7235 2351, extension 146).